IMAGES
of America

GLEN ROCK

"Our Rock has been very precious to us in Glen Rock. It came up in the ice age and our Lenni Lenape Indians met here for tribal ceremonies. Our Rock has been noted in old deeds. Our Rock has a magnetic strength and it has become our symbol. May it serve for centuries to come as our sign."—Mabel Hubschmitt, September 14, 1969, chairman of the 75th Anniversary Committee. (*The Sunday News,* "Glen Rock Anniversary," September 28, 1969.)

IMAGES
of America
GLEN ROCK

Diane Humphrey Barsa

ARCADIA
PUBLISHING

Published by Arcadia Publishing
Charleston, South Carolina

Library of Congress Catalog Card Number: 2002106381

For all general information contact Arcadia Publishing at:
Telephone 843-853-2070
Fax 843-853-0044
E-mail sales@arcadiapublishing.com
For customer service and orders:
Toll-Free 1-888-313-2665

Visit us on the Internet at www.arcadiapublishing.com

CONTENTS

ACKNOWLEDGMENTS

I want to extend my heartfelt thanks to the many people who shared their memories and photographs: Regina Aber, Robert and Dorthy Bassett, Dorothy Becica, Mary Ellen Betson, Helen M. Dages, Howard Dean, Lewis Dunham, Jane Edmondson, Robert Evans, Norma Hibbard, Paul and Diane Herrlett, Eileen Bushman Hoagland, Marjorie LaForge, Donna Smith Nihen, Jon Osborn, Richard B. Parker, Jean Seybolt Rey, Robert Sinkway, and Pamela Smith Speck.

I would also like to thank the Glen Rock Historical and Preservation Society (GRHPS) for access to its archives. Those archives contain the majority of photographs used for this publication. Over the years, many local organizations donated their records to the GRHPS and this allowed me to view years of records for events such as Independence Day Association (IDA) parades, school activities, and other town-wide events. Donations to the archives by the League of Women Voters of Glen Rock and the Glen Rock Public Library were invaluable in researching early history.

A thanks goes to Georgene Betterbed and Harriet Nardo Riley for assisting with the review of over 400 photographs.

I wish to acknowledge those who put to paper their knowledge, feelings, old stories, and daily thoughts regarding life in our town: Anthony Thurston, who wrote of daily life in his 1882 journal; George Hubschmitt, whose handwritten pages of Glen Rock history number in the hundreds; Mabel Hubschmitt, whose words are quoted in many documents regarding our borough; Lily Hubschmitt, who saved her family's photographs and ephemera; and Fred Arndt, who as a youth took his camera to town, giving us snapshots of life by documenting each photograph with subject, date, place, and time.

Last, my gratitude goes to my husband Raymond and son Raymond Jr. for allowing me the time and giving up the dining room and computer so that I was able to research, compile, and write.

INTRODUCTION

Native Americans were the first inhabitants of the area known as Glen Rock. The Lenni Lenape fished and hunted in heavily wooded areas. They used a trail from Hackensack to Arcola, then traveled past the Rock and up to Oakland, where they reached the Ramapo River. Stories have been passed down that tell of the Lenni Lenape council meetings on the Rock and the smoke signals that were sent from fires lit atop the Rock.

New Jersey Dutchmen were required to purchase land from agents who represented the General Board of Proprietors of the Eastern Division of New Jersey. Although not required, settlers also purchased deeds from the Lenni Lenape, beginning in the early 1700s. This may be why wars did not occur in the region between the settlers and Native Americans.

The Dutch used trails worn down by years of Native Americans traversing the hills and valleys. They cleared trees and created self-sufficient farms. Over the next 150 years, descendants of the early settlers built the majority of new farms and houses. The region, which included Glen Rock, Midland Park, Wortendyke, and Ridgewood, was referred to as Newtown. It was a part of Franklin Township.

The Rock was noted on some Revolutionary War maps and the area was familiar to the Continental Army. The British were also familiar with the region and were known for foraging.

Newtown was renamed Wortendyke in 1810. The name changed again in 1829 when Abraham Godwin, a war hero, was honored with the new name, Godwinville.

Perhaps the greatest change to the lives of the local residents between the founding of our country and the Civil War was the coming of the railroad in 1848. The single track brought goods and took local mill products and produce to markets. The mail was delivered in a leather bag brought by the train. By the mid-1850s, commuting to New York City was possible.

The men who went off to fight for the Union during the Civil War belonged to Companies B and D of the 22nd Regiment of the New Jersey Infantry, known as the Bergen County Regiment. They fought at Chancellorsville, Virginia, on May 2 and 3, 1863.

After the Civil War, city dwellers began to come to the area for the summers or long weekends. Godwinville was advertised as being malaria free and good for asthma and tuberculosis sufferers. Because the commute by train was not difficult, many families made permanent moves to the area.

In 1876, Franklin Township was split and Ridgewood Township came into existence. Glen Rock was formed from Ridgewood Township School District No. 44 and a portion of Saddle River Township.

The New Jersey Legislature passed a bill abolishing three-man school district boards that existed for each of the small school districts. Ridgewood elected a nine-man board that had to consolidate the schools. The one-room school faced extinction as graded schools were to be built. Ridgewood planned to close School No. 44, the Ridgewood-Grove School. Residents of the district went house to house along the line of District No. 44 and asked what each resident preferred, Ridgewood-Grove School or the proposed Beech Street School. The different opinions are still visible today in the zigzag border between the two towns. The area taken from Saddle River Township has a fairly straight border due to the large farms in the region.

This publication contains photographs that tell the story of how Glen Rock changed over time. Many images are of long-gone farms, mills, hotels, schools, trolleys, and trains. And many show people who helped to make Glen Rock what it is today. The first chapter, "Before There Was Glen Rock," includes some of the earliest photographs taken in Glen Rock. These photographs present a view of the rural setting and the early settlers' lives. The second chapter, "The Borough Is Born," focuses on early Glen Rock and the growth that occurred through World War I. The third chapter, "1920 through World War II," reflects the housing developments, centralization of the business district, and improved municipal services in Glen Rock. The final chapter, "Years of Growth: 1947 through 1959," shows the building and growth that occurred at this time, as many people moved here to enjoy suburban life.

One

BEFORE THERE WAS GLEN ROCK

Once, the Rock stood alone. Brought by the Wisconsin glacier from the Hudson Bay region over 15,000 years ago, it was deposited as the glacier receded at the end of the last ice age. The Lenni Lenape called it Pammackapuka, the meaning of which is debated. One translation is "large rock which fell from heaven." The second translation relates to the shape, "sweat house." The Rock is noted in several old documents including the Ramapo Patent of 1709, the Alexander and Morris Survey of 1763, and Revolutionary War maps.

This Dutch brownstone home of the Berdan family was built in 1712. The holdings included farmland, pastures, and woodlands on both sides of today's Lincoln Avenue in Glen Rock and Hawthorne. It ended at the famous rock in the north. A descendent of the Berdan family sold the house to George Goode in 1890. He passed it on to his son. In 1938, the house was demolished when state highway 208 was constructed.

The Marinus family farmhouse, built in the mid-1800s, was once surrounded by acres of corn. David Marinus was a farmer and mill owner. He was one of the first councilmen for Glen Rock. Franklin Marinus served as a member of the board for School No. 44. John Marinus was elected the first assessor for Glen Rock. When the land was sold and divided into lots, the house was left sitting alone near Diamond Brook and was demolished as the area around Boulevard was developed. Marinus Place and the Marinus Place Bridge over Diamond Brook carry the founding family name.

Alfred DeBaun and his family lived in this home on Cherry Lane (now Lincoln Avenue). The home was built in the 1850s. DeBaun was one of the first council members, elected to a two-year term in the first elections.

Two friends of the Hubschmitt family stop to adjust a hat while walking on Edwards Lane (now Hamilton Avenue) in the 1890s. Rocks lined the side of the lane that had homes on it. Sidewalks were made from wooden planks.

These are homes on Edwards Lane, east of Paterson Road (now Maple Avenue), as they appeared in 1890. The first was the home of the Mead family. Henry Mead cast one of the two "nay" votes against the creation of Glen Rock on September 14, 1894. Mead stated that he wanted to vote "yea," but feared a unanimous vote would be considered illegal. He became the third mayor of Glen Rock, serving from 1899 to 1900, on the borough's first Republican ticket. The second house was the Cobb family home and later became 203 Hamilton Avenue. The Charles Longsdorf family resided in the third home. These people are unidentified.

Jean Edwards rides her bicycle down Paterson Road on the way home from Ridgewood. The stone-and shrub-lined dirt road was heavily traveled by foot, bicycle, horse and buggy, and stagecoach. During the 1890s, bicyclists pressured civic officials to repair rutted roads. Glen Rock's first ordinance, after becoming incorporated, stated that bicycles were not to be on sidewalks and were not permitted "between sunset and sunrise on any street without carrying a lighted bicycle signal lamp…carrying a bicycle bell, gong, or horn…not exceeding the rate of eight miles an hour."

The Mead family had this view from their front porch. Edwards Lane is in front of the house. Rock Road, on the right, goes past the house and continues past trees and farmland. The hedge hides Paterson Road. The farmhouse on the corner of Paterson Road and Rock Road is the Courter homestead. This is the house where George, Lilly, and Mabel Hubschmitt were born. It is also where their mother, Fannie Courter, was born a generation earlier. Today, it is the site of the Glen Rock Public Library.

The Hopper Family Burying Ground is listed on the Bergen County Historical Society's Cemetery inventory. It is located on Spottswood Road where the farms of Garrett E. Hopper and Hendrick H. Hopper met. Descendants of Hendrick Jan Hopper are buried in the cemetery. The earliest burial is that of Peter Demarest, who died on February 26, 1804, at the age of six years. The latest burial is that of Eliza Westervelt Hopper, wife of Garret J. Hopper, who died on October 22, 1894, at the age of 68 years, 8 months, and 22 days. Years ago their tombstones, along with the 42 others in the cemetery, were placed flat within the ground to prevent damage.

This tombstone reads, "MEMORY OF JOHN H. HOPPER WHO DIED August 7, 1859: aged 71 years, 2 months and 7 days. This world is vain and full of pain/ With cares and troubles sore/ But they are blest who are at rest/ With Christ forevermore."

This tombstone reads, "ANN HOPPER DIED DEC. 27th 1888 AGED 74 YEARS 7 MONTHS & 17 DAYS—AT REST."

The Marinus family was one of the first to settle in the region, arriving in the mid-1700s. David J. Marinus built his woodworking mill in the 1870s. One of two mills located in the area, it was on the west bank of Diamond Brook in the vicinity of today's Boulevard. Marinus is sitting on the step before the door to the mill and an unidentified fisherman is sitting along the bank of the brook. The mill, which was torn down prior to the development of Boulevard, had

...f Rock Road, where it
..., the state mandated a
...d to build a new school
...arious meetings, a house-
...d if occupants wanted to
...lled South Ridgewood. A
...k. School No. 44 served the
...meeting hall for many years
...h are Jean Edwards (center)

...wheel were buried beneath
... and I went over to Mr.
... I took my hot bed sash
...ary, 1882."

17

Ridgewood-Grove School No. 44 was built in 1846 at the then end of
met the Godwinville-Hackensack Road (Ackerman Avenue). In 189
consolidation of school districts within townships. Ridgewood decide
more centrally located and to close School No. 44. In response, after
to-house survey was conducted by a handful of citizens. They aske
remain in Ridgewood or be a part of a new town, originally to be c
survey was completed and filed with the proper papers in Hackensac
new borough of Glen Rock until 1899. It continued to be a local
after and *still* exists as a private residence. In this 1890s photogra
and her cousins from Paterson.

Two

THE BOROUGH IS BORN

A young girl protects herself from the sun as she walks past the Rock and the four mailboxes located there in 1908. This picture belonged to Henry Carpenter Smith, a partner in the Smith-Singer Realty Company of Glen Rock, which played one of the most important roles in planning the community we enjoy today.

This is the Rock in winter. This view faces west towards today's Lincoln Avenue. Two chestnut trees grew alongside the Rock until blight killed them. A lone farmhouse stands down the road.

During its early years, the Smith-Singer Realty Company produced postcards to advertise Glen Rock. Formed in 1908, the company built approximately 700 homes and 21 stores in the borough. The Smith-Singer Realty Company dissolved in 1933. (Courtesy of Carolyn Blake.)

Life-long resident Lilly Hubschmitt stated in an April 1, 1981 interview with the *Suburban News*, "Not so much of the Rock was exposed as it is today." She recalled family outings around the Rock. She and her playmates would climb to the top with the aid of a chestnut tree. In this photograph, early Glen Rockers enjoyed outings around the Rock. ("Glen Rock, A Self Portrait," published by the League of Women Voters of Glen Rock, 1954. Photograph courtesy of F. John Walter.)

The original survey submitted to Hackensack referred to "SO. RIDGEWOOD." It was changed to Glen Rock at the last minute to avoid potential future confusion with Ridgewood. The first use of Glen Rock is credited to a long-ago area resident, Charles M. Veil. Eighty-two residents of the proposed borough voted. There were eighty "yea" votes and two "nays." The "nay" votes were cast to avoid any questions a unanimous election might bring. The Borough of Glen Rock was formed on September 14, 1894.

This cracker box was converted to the ballot box for the incorporation election and several of the municipal elections that followed. To count the vote, the ballot was removed from the ballot box, the checks on the ballot were counted, and it was placed in the envelope that was then added to others on a string.

The first municipal election was held on October 2, 1894, at Andrew V.D. Snyder's greenhouse at the corner of Paterson Road (Maple Avenue) and Highwood Avenue. The difference in the two tickets was due to concern regarding the best candidate for chosen freeholder.

Glen Rock Borough.
CITIZENS' TICKET.

For Mayor,
ANDREW V. D. SNYDER.

For Councilman, 1 year,
DAVID J. MARINUS,
GARRET T. HOPPER.

For Councilmen, 2 years,
ALFRED DEBAUN,
RICHARD T. SNYDER.

For Councilmen, 3 years.
JOHN A. ACKERMAN,
JOHN J. TERHUNE.

For Chosen Freeholder,
HENRY DEMAREST.

For Assessor,
JOHN A. MARINUS.

For Collector,
JOHN B. VAN DERBECK.

For Commissioners of Appeals,
EDWARD BARTON,
HENRY D. ALYEA,
NICHOLAS D. HOPPER.

RESOLVED, That the sum of $600. be raised for borough purposes.

Glen Rock Borough.
INDEPENDENT TICKET.

For Mayor,
RICHARD T. SNYDER.

For Councilman, 1 year,
DAVID J. MARINUS,
GARRET T. HOPPER.

For Councilmen, 2 years,
ALFRED DEBAUN,
HENRY DEMAREST.

For Councilmen, 3 years.
JOHN A. ACKERMAN,
JOHN J. TERHUNE.

For Chosen Freeholder,
ANDREW V. D. SNYDER.

For Assessor,
JOHN A. MARINUS.

For Collector,
JOHN B. VAN DERBECK.

For Commissioners of Appeals,
EDWARD BARTON,
HENRY D. ALYEA,
NICHOLAS D. HOPPER.

RESOLVED, That the sum of $600. be raised for borough purposes.

The Independent ticket was created to allow Andrew Snyder to be elected chosen freeholder. His cousin, Richard, was changed from a candidate for councilman to mayor. Henry Demarest was changed from being the candidate for chosen freeholder to councilman. The ticket was elected. The $600 raised through the resolution was used for the first administrative expenses and roads.

JOHN J. STORMS,

DEALER IN

Marble and Granite Monuments, Head Stones, etc.

CEMETERY WORK.

Ridgewood, N. J., April 2 1896

Glen Rock Borough to

John J. Storms Dr

Puting up Booths delivering
Ballot Box and taking down
Booths posting notices
of Election $3.00

Received Payment

John J. Storms

State of New Jersey
County of Bergen

John J Storms being duly
Sworn on his oath says the above is just and
true Sworn and subscribed before me
this 2d day of April 1896 John J. Storms
Richard J. Snyder
Mayor

The ballot box was used many times over the years. A local stonecutter and cemetery worker, John Storms, was paid to set up voting booths, deliver the ballot box, and then dismantle the booths.

DEMOCRATIC TICKET.
Glen Rock Borough.

For Member of the House of Representatives of the United States, Sixth District:
WILLIAM HUGHES.

For Members of the General Assembly:
CHARLES F. THOMPSON,

JAMES S. HART.

For Chosen Freeholder:
JACOB D. VAN EMBURGH, JR.

For Collector, 2 years:
JACOB J. MAY.

For Councilmen, 3 years:
GEORGE PHILLIPS.

JOHN W. COURTER.

Appropriations:
For Borough purposes, $400.
For repair of roads, $200.
For road improvements, $800.

NATIONAL PROHIBITION TICKET.
Glen Rock Borough.

For Member of the House of Representatives of the United States, Sixth District:
HERBERT W. COLLINGWOOD.

For Members of the General Assembly:
ARCHIBALD C. WORTH,

ANDREW J. DE VOE.

For Chosen Freeholder:

For Collector (2 years):

For Councilmen (3 years):

The diversity of political beliefs is reflected in these four tickets from the 1906 election. The Democratic ticket was elected in Glen Rock.

SOCIALIST TICKET.
Glen Rock Borough.

For Member of the House of Representatives of the United States, Sixth District:
CHARLES P. DE YOE.

For Members of the General Assembly:
CHARLES TURRIAN,

PHILIPP KAMMERER.

For Chosen Freeholder:

For Collector (2 years):

For Councilmen (3 years):

REPUBLICAN TICKET.
Glen Rock Borough.

For Member of the House of Representatives of the United States, Sixth District:
GEORGE H. BURKE.

For Members of the General Assembly:
JAMES DE VINE, JR.,

GUY L. FAKE.

For Chosen Freeholder:
CORNELIUS P. CROUTER.

For Collector, 2 years:
PETER VAN WINKLE.

For Councilmen, 3 years:
NELSON S. CUBBERLY,

ALBERT VANDENBERG.

Appropriations:
For Borough purposes, $400.
For repair of roads, $200.
For road improvements, $800.

Ridgewood-Grove School No. 44 was last used as a school in 1899. These are the last children to attend school in the Red Brick Schoolhouse. Seen here are, from left to right, as follows: (first row) Jeanette May, Mary Van Den Berg, two unidentified girls, Elsie Youngsman, unidentified, John Streelman, Kenneth Jones, Raymond Newton, ? Montress, and two unidentified boys; (second row) unidentified, Edward Phillips, and unidentified; (third row) ? Frazer, Sadie Youngsman, Jennie Van Den Berg, Emma Marinus, Jennie Borman, unidentified, Katie Katz, E. Phillips, unidentified, George Doremus, Chester Jones, and two unidentified boys; (fourth row) Mamie Lynch, Margaret Van Den Berg, Henrietta De Young, Mamie Ward, Jemima Zabriskie, Effah Montress, Jacob Van Den Berg, and three unidentified boys; (fifth row) Agnes Snyder, Alfred Van Den Berg, William Eagan, Fred Montress, Mr. Charles P. Carter (teacher), Thomas Ackerman, and unidentified.

On land purchased for $600, this four-room school, known as School No. 1, was built for $3,400 and opened its doors in 1900. Charles Carter was both the principal and a teacher. Maud Christopher was the second teacher. Approximately 75 students were registered. The building had a hot-air furnace and an artesian well with a pump in the rear yard.

Due to increased enrollment, two more classrooms and two additional teachers were added in 1903. The students attended grades one through eight.

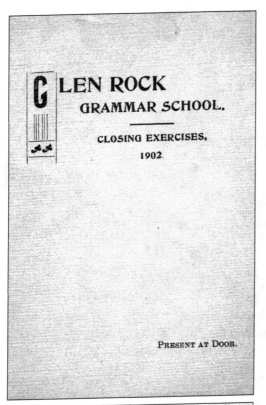

Graduating from the Glen Rock Grammar School was an event, even when only two students matriculated. Graduates of the grammar school, wanting to further their education, attended Ridgewood High School.

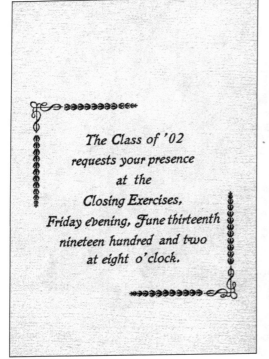

An unidentified teacher and students of School No. 1 are pictured here in 1911.

This is the fourth-grade class of School No. 1 in 1914.

Year 1912
12-13

Grade 3

Glen Rock School

Pupil Mabel Hubschmitt Teacher Edith L. Christopher

MONTH	Days Present	Days Absent	Tardy	Deportment	Reading	Writing	Spelling	Arithmetic	Drawing	Language	Geography	History	Current History	Algebra	Physiology	Etymology	Business Forms	Civil Government			General Average	PARENT'S SIGNATURE
September	19				G	G	E	E	VG	G	E	VG	VG			VG					VG	A. T. Hubschmitt
October	20	3			G	F	E	E	E	P						VG					VG	A. T. Hubschmitt
November	18				VG	G	E	E	G	VG	E					E					VG	A. Hubschmitt
December	15				VG	G	E	E	G	G	G					E					VG	A. Hubschmitt
January	11	9			E	G	E	93	97	VG	98					E					VG	E. T. Hubschmitt
February	18	1			E	G	E	E	G	VG	E					E					VG	A. T. Hubschmitt
March	19½	½			VG	G	E	E	VG	G	E					E					VG	A. T. Hubschmitt
April	22				VG	G	E	E	E	E	E					E					E	A. T. Hubschmitt
May	20½	½			E	G	E	E	VG	VG	E					E					VG	A. T. Hubschmitt
June	10				E	VG	E	100	95	VG	99					E					E	A. T. Hubschmitt
Average	17³	126			14	da absent																A. S. Hubschmitt
Final					173	da pres.																

Promoted

Standing in Studies and Deportment, viz: 100 Perfect, 90 Very Good, 80 Good, 70 Fair, 60 Poor.

PECKHAM, LITTLE & CO., SCHOOL SUPPLIES, NEW YORK.

The Glen Rock School used Union Monthly Report Cards. This is the final report card for Mabel Hubschmitt's year as a third-grade student.

School No. 1 was often a place of fun. Here, photograph-viewing machines have been set up in the back of the school during a borough-wide Fourth of July celebration. The building on the left is the original firehouse. (Courtesy of Eileen Bushman Hoagland.)

Holiday greetings were sent to borough officials and the families of students. Maud Christopher's 40 students are listed on the Christmas greeting below.

Names of Pupils.

Percy Ackerman	Olive Ferguson
Nachur Alnemy	George C. Hubschmitt
Frank Alnemy	Chester Jones
Lena Alnemy	H. Kenneth Jones
Jessie Alyea	LeRoy May
Archie Burrows	Nettie May
Katie Bergman	Hudson May
Margaret Bassett	Florence McGill
John Coombs	Raymond Montress
Morris T. Cubberley	Carrie C. Ochs
Ethel Cubberley	Edward E. Phillips
James Curtin	George Phillips
Timothy Curtin	Lillian Putnam
Mildred Christopher	Nora Storms
Fleta Christopher	Harry Santhouse
Bessie Courter	Floyd Snyder
Harold C. Demarest	Mary Van Den Berg
George Doremus	Olen Van Blarcom
Edna Edwards	Jennie Vanden Berg
Annie Faber	Elsie Youngsman

Graduation Exercises

of the

Glen Rock Grammar School

Wednesday, June 27, 1917, 8 P. M.

Glen Rock, New Jersey

BOARD OF EDUCATION

Charles P. Van Allen, *President*
Frank B. Ellis, *Vice President*
Henry C. Smith

Arthur White
Peter Ebbert
Flourence Baur

William D. Murphy
Charles P. MacGill
John W. Courter

George F. Moody, *Principal*

Albert M. Fowler, *Secretary*

The graduation exercises of 1917 were postponed due to an outbreak of scarlet fever. When held, the program began with the school chorus singing "Columbia My Motherland." Readings by graduates included "America a World Power," "Mexico the Land of Unrest," "Who's Afraid," "Constantius and the Lion," and "The Origins of Beethoven's Moonlight Sonata." Piano solos began with *Moonlight Sonata* and included *Electra* and *The Fountain*. A scene from *The Merchant of Venice* was presented by five of the graduates. The chorus sang "Blow Soft Winds," and, after the presentations of diplomas, ended the program with the song "Barcarolle."

The class of 1917 is identified, from left to right, as follows: (front row) unidentified and Bruce Ellis; (second row) Ruth Jeffries, unidentified, Anthony Thurston, Ethel Wright (teacher), William Zabriskie, Norman Marinus, and Mabel Hubschmitt; (third row) Irma Rider, Henrietta Soodsma, unidentified, Jeannette More, Alice Simons, unidentified, Janet Somerville, and Esther Longstreet.

School No. 2 was dedicated in 1915. Originally four classrooms, an addition was completed in 1931. At that time, the name was changed to the Richard E. Byrd School. A second addition was completed in 1958. (*Ridgewood Herald Illustrated Supplement*, January 2, 1919. Courtesy of Regina Aber.)

In the *1876 Atlas of Bergen County New Jersey*, this building is listed as J. Smith, Bowling Green Inn. Located on the southwest corner of Paterson Road (Maple Avenue) and Rock Road, *c.* 1900 it changed owners and was then known as the Old Half-Way House. It changed owners again a few years later and is still remembered by some long-time residents as the Garrabrant Hotel. According to the April 30, 1913 issue of the *Glen Rock Observer*, John R. Garrabrant died on April 25 and "rested in an oak casket in the parlor of the hotel." Garrabrant's son was mayor at the time. The noisy establishment was gutted by fire soon after the beginning of Prohibition. It was totally demolished in the mid-1930s.

Abe Christopher's blacksmith shop was located on the corner of Paterson Road and Rock Avenue (Maple Avenue and South Highwood Avenue). This photograph was taken in 1905. Christopher was the town marshall, appointed on June 6, 1895. He was not salaried, but he was paid for each arrest that he made.

The Smith-Singer Building was built on the corner of Rock Road and Main Street in 1912. The original occupants were a land development company. The Smith-Singer Company (organized in 1908 by Henry C. Smith and Dr. John G. Singer) was located here and rented space to John Geils' Grocery and Simone Iudica's shoemaking store. The land and the acres around the building were wooded with birch trees that can be seen in the background.

By 1913, the birch trees were replaced by homes built by the Smith-Singer Company. From 1913 until 1929, the borough leased a portion of the Smith-Singer Building that was used as the clerk's office, police station, and jail. The assembly hall on the second floor was used for various municipal meetings, as well as for parties, recitals, fundraisers, and festive activities. The third floor had two apartments. A fire on November 15, 1973, destroyed the third floor, and it was never rebuilt.

By 1920, a two-story addition was built alongside the Smith-Singer Building. The first floor housed the Great Eastern Store. The second floor had two apartments.

Within a short time, De Korte's Market was located on the corner of Main Street and Rodney Street, in the addition to the Smith-Singer Building. The library occupied space behind the bakery from 1922 to 1925. (Courtesy of Mr. and Mrs. Jim Miller.)

Coombs Confectionery opened on Rock Road early in the 1900s. Percy Coombs, the gentleman on the left, owned the store. His son, John Bryant Coombs, is looking out of the upstairs window. Next door is Wentink Watchmaker and Jeweler. (Courtesy of Jennie Coombs, widow of John Bryant Coombs.)

First National Bank of Glen Rock and Hubbard Real Estate were the original occupants in the building that still stands at the southeast corner of Rock Road and the Bergen Line. (Courtesy of Ridgewood Public Library.)

Andrew Van Dien Snyder founded Snyder's Greenhouse in 1886. It was located at the northwest corner of Paterson Road (Maple Avenue) and Highwood Avenue. The borough's first election was held at the greenhouse. Snyder's son, Andrew J. Snyder, took over the business upon the elder's death in 1918. Pictured above are Harry Sinkway and Andrew J. Snyder. (Courtesy of Robert Sinkway.)

The Smith-Singer Realty Company had this building-materials warehouse beside the Main Line tracks, just north of Rock Road. The houses that the company built were rented for the first year in order to allow prospective buyers time to see if they liked the home and Glen Rock. When Ida Faber's family decided to purchase a home, the down payment was an organ. (Oral interview with Ida Faber, Glen Rock Historical Society records.)

Peter Van Winkle built these coops for his chickens prior to 1912. He was the tax collector during the early 1900s, and he was available at his residence on South Maple Avenue each weekday between 9:00 a.m. and 2:00 p.m. Annual taxes were due by December 20th.

John W. Courter was born in the 1870s
in what is now Glen Rock. The family's
homestead was on the corner of Paterson
Road (Maple Avenue) and Rock Road,
where the Glen Rock Public Library is
now located.

An auction day was a social event. The Vandenberg farm was auctioned off in 1911. It was located
between Ackerman Avenue and Prospect Street, in the area of today's East Gramercy.

David Courter and Richard De Young were farmers in Glen Rock. Courter's homestead was on Paterson Road (Maple Avenue) and Rock Road. De Young's farm was between Ackerman Avenue and Prospect Street, in the area of Rock Road. Courter had a cow, some chickens, and grew vegetables. De Young had 55 acres where he ran a dairy and raised horses, pigs, and poultry. In addition, De Young served as mayor from 1932 to 1935. This photograph shows the two men taking produce to market in Paterson.

This is the first motor vehicle used in Glen Rock to transport produce to the New York markets. It was photographed in 1911. Barney Smith stands beside his truck, which is laden with cabbage and corn. His farm was located in the area of today's East Gramercy and Prospect Street.

These unidentified riders are in a wicker buggy with a fringed top. The horse is decorated with fringed equipment. The road is dirt, kept level by local men.

Glen Rock, N. J., Nov. 2 1896

THE MAYOR AND COUNCIL OF THE BOROUGH OF GLEN ROCK,

To David A. Courter Dr.

for road work

Address, Ridgewood

Sept.	4	1 day work on road				1	50
"	5	½ " " " "					75
"	7	1 " " " " "				1	50
"	8	1 " " " " "				1	50
"	9	1 " " " " "				1	50
"	10	1 " " " " "				1	50
"	11	1 " " " " "				1	50

Received, Nov. 5 , 1896, from Treasurer of Borough of Glen Rock $9. 75
in full settlement of above claim.
David, A. Courter

David Courter was one of many men who supplemented their farm income by working on local roads.

A couple poses on the bridge where Rock Road passes over Diamond Brook. Wagon wheel ruts show that some chose not to use the bridge. The wooden plank was another alternative.

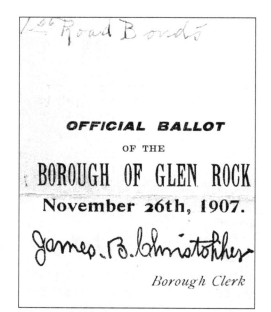

OFFICIAL BALLOT

OF THE

BOROUGH OF GLEN ROCK

November 26th, 1907.

James B. Christopher

Borough Clerk

BOROUGH OF GLEN ROCK

—

SPECIAL ELECTION

—

AGAINST

the issue of Thirty-five Thousand Dollars of Bonds, according to the Resolution of the Council, dated October 8th, 1907.

Glen Rock's first road bond was voted upon on November 26, 1907. The measure passed, and in 1908 Rock Road, Prospect Street, Ackerman Avenue, and Lincoln Avenue were paved. Attempts were made to raise additional funds to pave the remaining dusty roads by placing added taxes on automobiles and each passenger. The attempts failed.

Broad Street was properly named, as it was one of the widest in the area. This 1918 view is looking north from Ackerman Avenue. Note the shadows of the camera and photographer in the lower right-hand corner.

Rock Road looking West, Glen Rock, N. J.

Postcards of Glen Rock were popular in the early 1900s. This view of Rock Road and the Hubschmitt house was taken in 1911. Lilly Hubschmitt noted on the back of the card that the trees around the house were pear. Electricity, sidewalks, and curbs give the appearance of a modern 1911 community, but note that the streets are dirt.

Horses and buggies were the most popular form of family transportation. The horses have fringed equipment. The riders are unidentified.

The "Edwards ladies, April 17, 1898," is noted on the back of this photograph. They were walking on the Cubberly tract. Property owners kept the roads adjoining their property lined with large stones. Many lined their section of road with trees and shrubs.

The Albertype Company of Brooklyn, New York, made dozens of postcards of the Glen Rock area. This card of the birch trees at the corner of South Maple and Ackerman Avenues was sold at E.W. Cobb Stationery in Ridgewood. Note the horse and buggy behind the trees on the left. (Courtesy of Howard Dean, descendent of E.W. Cobb.)

By horse and buggy or by walking, Glen Rock parishioners attended the borough's first church, the Reformed Church. The church began when Rev. J.A. Van Neste of the Classis of Paramus noted, at a meeting held in Warwick, New York, in October of 1895, that a committee should study the need for a church in Glen Rock. By December, the first consistory meeting was held in the home of George Hopper. Soon, land was purchased from Henry Mead and men began building. On April 11, 1896, the church incorporation was recorded in the Bergen County clerk's office. The building was completed by November 1896. Services were held in the church beginning in late 1896. The interior of the church was finished during the following year, and the church was dedicated in 1898. Today, the Glen Rock Community Church stands on this site.

Homes were built along South Maple Avenue during the early 1900s. This 1910 photograph is of homes across from School No. 1. The Reformed Church can be seen in the distance.

The Bungalow Street.   GLEN ROCK, N. J.

Penny postcards advertised bungalow-style homes that were built throughout the borough before World War I. Builders left some birch trees on each lot. (Courtesy of Robert Evans.)

Louis Van Winkle owned the first automobile in Glen Rock. His bright red 1910 Brush had one cylinder and two speeds, as well as brass oil lamps for night driving.

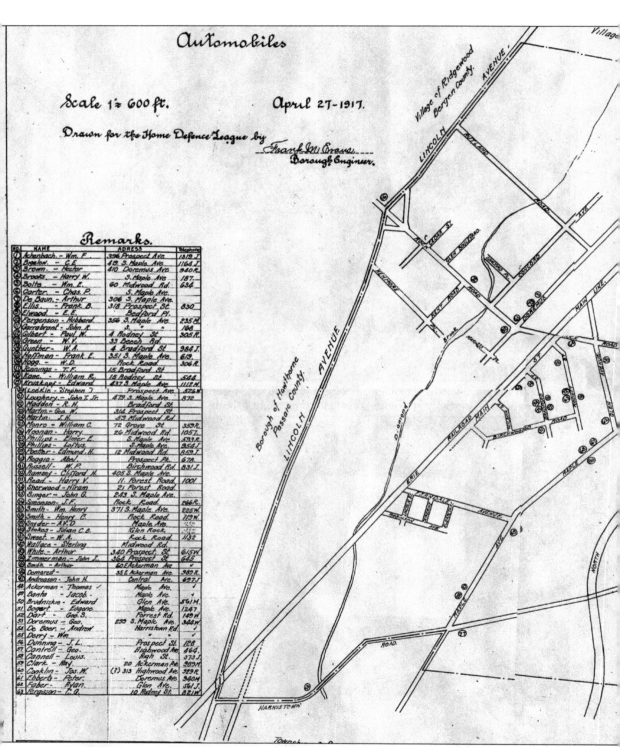

By 1917, there were 85 automobiles in town. At the request of the Home Defense League, Frank M. Evans, the borough engineer, drew this map showing the locations and owners of

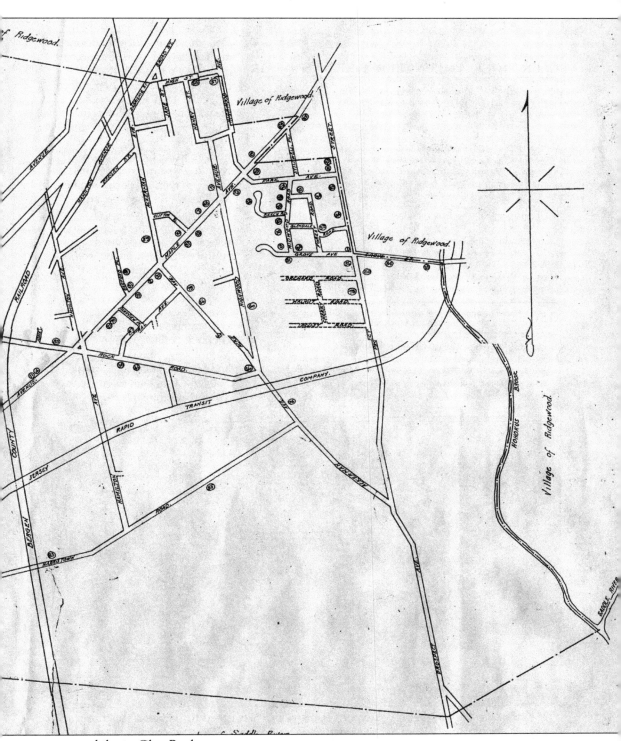

automobiles in Glen Rock.

GLEN ROCK VOLUNTEER FIREMAN'S FAIR

THURSDAY, DECEMBER 15, 6 to 11 P. M.
FRIDAY, DECEMBER 16, 6 to 11 P. M.
SATURDAY, DECEMBER 17, 2 to 11 P. M.

"All the world loves a—Fireman"

HE object of this Fair is to provide equipment for the recently organized Glen Rock Volunteer Fire Co., a necessity so urgent and laudable that all should contribute to its success. The many unique and original features outlined in this program assure an enjoyable time to all who participate. The Fireman's Booth will be particularly attractive, appealing to all Firemen and their friends. Read about the Old Fashioned Country Store. Read everything!

There will be all kinds of bargains for the ladies and plenty of ways for the men to spend a nickel or two; but there will be fair dealing and remarkable values for all.

Recently elected State and County officials are expected to attend and may tell us why they were elected and what they will do.

35c Special Supper every night 6 to 8 o'clock served by **35c**
GARRABRANT

Visiting Firemen will be served at any hour. Thursday, ROAST. Friday, OYSTER. Saturday, CHICKEN. Everyone knows what this means, so bring your appetite and your pocketbook. Light refreshments also.

Have you heard about that $400 house lot? Free conveyance from Tice's every half hour, 6 to 9 o'clock. Also from Edwards Lane trolley station.

The Glen Rock Volunteer Fire Department was first mentioned at the October 11, 1909 meeting of the town council. It was officially founded on September 27, 1910. In lieu of a special election to approve funds for equipment, for three days that December a Fireman's Fair was held at School No. 1. Supper was provided by Garrabrant's Inn. The families of the firemen, Women's Civic League, and Glen Rock Progress Circle sponsored booths. A Japanese tea garden, old-fashioned country store, lemonade well, and art gallery were created. A theatrical program consisted of a one-act comedy sketch, "The Sweet Family" and vaudeville-type entertainment, including "Popular ballads, Italian Monologue, The Banjo King, and Fancy Dancing." (Official Souvenir Program, Glen Rock Volunteer Fireman's Fair.)

The funds raised at the 1910 Volunteer Fireman's Fair were used to purchase this fire truck, delivered on July 3, 1911. The headquarters were located beside School No. 1, at Maple Avenue and Van Allen Road. Horses could not be kept just for the purpose of fighting fires, and the volunteers depended upon whatever animals were available when an alarm sounded.

The original 1911 fire truck was motorized in 1917 with funds raised through dances held at the Smith-Singer Assembly Hall.

This 1913 photograph is of one of the three steel locomotive tires that served as fire alarms during the early years of the borough. Seen here are, from left to right, Carrie C. Ochs, Mabel Hubschmitt, and Florence L. Hallock. In 1919, a siren in the tower of School No. 1 replaced the locomotive tires. A restored steel locomotive tire, dedicated to William Maynard, the borough's first historian, now stands in Triangle Park.

This 1918 photograph shows that maneuvering the older roads in town had become more and more difficult. They were in disrepair, and the newer developments had graded streets.

New homes and old farms coexisted in Glen Rock. Many families kept chickens, children had animal husbandry projects through scouting, and truck farms supplied fresh produce to locals. (Courtesy of Marjorie LaForge.)

New homes were built in several areas of the borough. Development in the area of Doremus Avenue and Rock Road caused controversy regarding the Rock. Developers wanted to destroy the Rock, which was apparently in their way. The borough's residents won the battle, and the Rock was excavated, stones were placed under part of it, and a sidewalk was built around it.

At the other end of town, Midwood Road was lined with stone gutters, some of which still exist. This area was referred to as the Prospect Park development. Years earlier, in 1907, a part of Garret Hopper's farm was purchased, and the developers attempted to get Edmund Wakelee, state senator, to sponsor a bill that would have Ridgewood annex Glen Rock. On Election Day, the bill was defeated by eight votes. (Courtesy of Howard Dean, descendent of E.W. Cobb.)

Glen Rock became a convenient home for commuters to New York City. The Erie Railroad ran the Main Line since the 1850s. Once mainly freight, by the 1890s there were nine people commuting to work each day. The station was built in 1905.

In 1881, the Erie Railroad purchased the Bergen County Railroad. From then on, passengers were given a daily choice of routes leaving from two different stops in Glen Rock. This photograph, dated July 20, 1913, shows Glen Rockers waiting for a Bergen Line train.

Electric and telephone lines ran alongside the railroad tracks. By 1912, there were 35 telephones in the borough.

Smith-Singer Company developers created this park area in 1915. In 1921, they offered the property to the borough for $10,000. After some negotiations, Main Street Park was established. The park still exists on Main Street, but the bandstand blew down in a storm many years ago. It was renamed Veteran's Park in 2002.

The North Jersey Rapid Transit Company began to lay electric trolley tracks and line through Glen Rock in 1908. A ramp and concrete pillars created the Glen Rock Viaduct that extended northward from Harristown Road and over the Erie Railroad's Bergen Line tracks by 1910. It continued to Suffern by the end of 1911. The train seen in this 1911 photograph is believed to be a "Sunday School Special." (*Interurban Interlude*, Comdr. E.J. Quinby, 1968.)

July 21, 1911, was to be motorman William Hutchinson's last day. He had resigned the day before, but the head of the organization, Francis Pilgrim, had asked him to work one more day. A summer storm came through and the lightning took out the power to some of the signals. Pilgrim and trackman, John Frotaillo, set out to repair the signals, heading southbound from Ridgewood. Hutchinson and the conductor, Jacob Freidman, were northbound from East Paterson. John Smith was in his father's cornfields (where East Gramercy now runs), checking to see if any corn was ready to go to market. Just a few months after completing the line to Suffern, the two trolleys crashed head on at a blind curve between Grove and Prospect Streets. Smith witnessed the disaster. Pilgrim, Hutchinson, and Frotaillo were killed. Dozens were injured. In order to settle lawsuits, the New Jersey Rapid Transit Company sold land that was to have been used for future expansion. In this photograph, construction engineer George Jackson Jr. examines the scene. The trolley discontinued service on New Year's Day, 1929, without prior notice. (*Interurban Interlude*, Comdr. E.J. Quinby, 1968.)

The Glen Rock Civic League held its second annual banquet on February 22, 1913, in the Smith-Singer Assembly Hall. The organization was formed in 1912, with the goal of creating a borough hall. The borough was using a leased portion of the Smith-Singer Building.

In this 1914 photograph, George Hubschmitt is walking with his team of horses in the Fourth of July Parade.

The competitive barrel roll on the grounds of School No. 1 was photographed on July 4, 1914.

After the 1918 Fourth of July Parade, booths on the grounds of School No. 1 were available to all who wanted to spend the afternoon eating and playing games. (Courtesy of Eileen Bushman Hoagland.)

The 1918 Children's Parade was well attended. Glen Rock youth dressed to match the parade's theme. (Courtesy of Eileen Bushman Hoagland.)

Three

1920 THROUGH WORLD WAR II

Veterans' Day, May 30, 1921, was the day Glen Rock remembered its five young men who had lost their lives during World War I. Since October 1917, there had been much discussion in town regarding how to honor the men serving in World War I. Various options, such as a memorial in Triangle Park, or renaming a school or building, were considered. It was decided that the Rock was an appropriate place for a bronze plaque.

Two-year-old Catherine Ebbert was chosen to unveil the memorial plaque honoring the veterans of World War I. She was the daughter of Glen Rock's first casualty of the war, Peter Ebbert. Ebbert's widow, Marion, was pregnant with Catherine when he was killed.

Local Boy Scouts participated in the unveiling of the memorial plaque.

The LaForge family members pose by the Rock on September 11, 1923. (Courtesy of Marjorie LaForge.)

This late-1920s postcard states that Glen Rock is "The Town That Makes New Jersey Famous." No reason for this claim to fame is given.

The site for a municipal building was debated for several years. A developer and a borough committee wanted the same site. Borough resident Dennis Kennelly bought the land and held it without profit until the citizens voted to purchase the property and construct a borough hall in 1928. The Smith-Singer Company issued this postcard.

Volunteer firemen from Glen Rock proudly rode in Ridgewood's Fourth of July Parade in 1930.

The newest in emergency services is shown to Glen Rock residents at a Fourth of July festival on the Central School grounds.

The borough's police force had grown over the years. The men in this 1930 photograph are identified, from left to right, as follows: (front row) Mayor Henry Smith and Chief Houlihan; (back row) Sam Jensen, Roy Finn, Samuel Parks, Cornelius Meyers, John Faber Sr., and John Mullqueen.

In this 1931 photograph, Charles Kolesar is leaning on a water pump beside the home he built at 377 Harristown Road. The man in the background is unidentified. (Courtesy of Jon Osborn, who received the photograph from William Austin, Charles Kolesar's son-in-law.)

On Saturday, August 18, 1938, Fred Arndt took a walk with his camera. The 15-year-old recorded that at 10:30 that morning this is how the corner of Harristown Road and Hamilton Avenue appeared. (Donated by Norma Hibbard, Fred Arndt's sister.)

On January 14, 1939, Fred Arndt took his camera to town. He recorded that at 11:15 a.m. he took this photograph of Ray Hauschild at Rock Road, near Glen Avenue. (Donated by Norma Hibbard, Fred Arndt's sister.)

Arndt then walked over to Kavner's on Rock Road and climbed to the roof of the garage. At 11:25 a.m. he recorded that this photograph was taken of Glen Avenue, near Rock Road, "in back of our house." The house on the right is where the post office now stands. (Donated by Norma Hibbard, Fred Arndt's sister.)

Winter's snow, 1920, covers the grounds of School No. 1. The bell, then located in the tower and heard all over town, is all that remains of the school. Purchased by Mr. and Mrs. Harrison Ackerman, it was donated to Central School and now resides in the school's entrance lobby.

The second-grade students of School No. 1 in 1921 all folded their hands for this photograph. (Courtesy of Robert Bassett, third row, ninth from the left.)

Several School No. 1 students line up for a photograph in 1925.

In 1931, School No. 2 was renovated. The name was then changed to the Richard E. Byrd School, in honor of the explorer. This postcard was sold at Kavner's Stationery store in town.

CENTRAL SCHOOL OF GLEN ROCK
NEW JERSEY

Central School was dedicated on Wednesday, April 7, 1926. This program for the dedication exercises lists events, which included selections by the Glen Rock School Band, an invocation by Rev. William J. Lonsdale, the presentation of the flag by the Junior Order of American Mechanics, and the presentation of a Bible by Rev. John E. Bailey on behalf of the Sunday schools of the Community Church and All Saints' Episcopal Chapel. Various speeches were given and board of education president, Bertrand Noble, presented the key to the school to Mayor Henry J. Woltman.

Central School, built as an elementary school, served as the junior high school during the 1930s, after Ridgewood lost two grade schools to fire and could no longer accept Glen Rock students in its junior high school. The elementary school students returned to School No. 1. Graduates of Central School then went to Ridgewood High School, a private high school, or trade school to further their educations. This is a 1932 photograph of the eighth grade. (Courtesy of Dorthy Verduin Bassett, bottom row, second from the left.)

The Central School Junior High had many activities, baseball being one of the favorites. Seen here are, from left to right, as follows: (first row) Buddy Ramsy; (second row) ? Duckberry, Bill Wagner, Garry May, Augie Bender, and Melvon Morrow; (third row) Bud Gripphes, ? Phillip, Walt Raffett, "Coach," Frank Kilroy, Dave Fisher, Ernney Alexander, and ? Buroma. (Courtesy of Robert Bassett.)

The 1932 Central School Junior High Band posed for this photograph outside of the entrance to the school. (Courtesy of Dorthy Verduin Bassett, first row, sixth from the left.)

Over the years, the Central School Junior High Band grew. The band participated in local events and school presentations.

This trophy was awarded to the Glen Rock Harmonica Band and reads, "The Albert N. Hoxie Award, Harmonica Contest, Philadelphia, 1929."

The Glen Rock Harmonica Band was formed in the late 1920s. Seen here is the 1928–1929 band. Principal Sooy brought in a German gentleman to teach the harmonica. The organization of the performing group gave students an opportunity to travel to New York City to play over the radio, compete throughout New Jersey and Pennsylvania, and perform in the Ridgewood Playhouse. Principal Sooy took students on hikes during the weekends, and all would bring their harmonicas.

At 5:10 p.m. on January 22, 1939, Fred Arndt took this photograph of the construction of the junior high school at Harristown Road and Hamilton Avenue. The school was built with federal Works Progress Administration funds. (Donated by Norma Hibbard, Arndt's sister.)

On opening day in 1939, the junior high school students at Central School marched down Hamilton Avenue to their new school building.

The religious communities in the borough grew as fast as the schools. The 1896 Reformed Church had become the Community Church. In 1920, the stucco church replaced the wooden structure and served until 1950.

On All Saints' Day, November 1919, the sanctuary for All Saints' Episcopal Church was consecrated. The church had been formed in 1913 and had grown over the years. By 1922, it had its first rector, Rev. John E. Bailey.

Ryan's Market was at the corner of Park and Maple Avenues. The site was built *c.* 1890 as a bakery, then the only store in what was to become Glen Rock. By 1904, it was run by William Christopher as a candy and tobacco store. This 1922 photograph is of the grocery store owner, Michael Ryan (right), and an employee who was the butcher.

The Home Service Station on Rock Road and Glen Avenue was built in the early 1920s. This postcard was produced for advertising.

In 1928, Frank Kilroy Jr. stood for this photograph in front of his father's original Kilroy's Wonder Store on South Maple Avenue. Beside it was White's Service Station, and further down was Garrabrant's Half-Way House. Frank "Pop" Kilroy displayed fruit and vegetables under the awning. Kilroy, or one of his two assistants, William Eckert and William Stubbs, prepared customers' orders. Until World War II, drivers in one of three red Diamond T trucks would deliver orders, unpack them, and collect the money from customers. In 1933, the store received a liquor license and became the first in Bergen County to sell frozen food. Frank Jr. took over the business in 1946. In 1954, the Wonder Market opened on Rock Road. Today, the original store is the borough annex, and White's Gulf is where Kilroy's offices are located.

Young photographer Fred Arndt took this photograph of Rock Road, looking west, on June 6, 1938, at 4:58 p.m. (Donated by Norma Hibbard, Arndt's sister.)

From the Rock, this was the view looking east on Rock Road in 1939.

Standing at the corner of Valley Road, this was the view looking east down Rock Road in 1939.

Notice the flagman's shanty, the small building to the right of the automobile, in this 1939 photograph of Rock Road at the Erie Railroad crossing. Flagmen had been located at the crossings since 1918. Between 7:00 a.m. and 7:00 p.m., the flagman would come out of the shanty and stop traffic when a train was approaching. Electric gates were not installed until the early 1950s.

The Main Line and the Bergen County Line both operated with steam engines until the 1950s. Lanterns lighted some cars. The brakeman applied the brakes by hand. The travel time from Glen Rock to the end of the line in Hoboken was approximately 30 minutes.

The Arrow Bus Line provided service to local towns. This 1926 view, which looks east down Ackerman, was taken at the corner of Maple and Ackerman Avenues.

The New Jersey Rapid Transit Company's electric trolley operated until 1929 when, without warning, it ceased business, leaving morning commuters wondering where the trolley was.

The trolley tracks were disassembled and sold to the builders of the Trans-Siberian Railroad. All that remained of the once-popular route was the trestle between Glen and Hamilton Avenues. A portion of it remains in the right of way, south of Wilde Park.

Roads were constantly being improved throughout the borough. In the 1930s, the creation of underpasses eliminated the railroad crossings at Maple Avenue by Glen Avenue and Ackerman Avenue at Broad Street. This photograph shows the Ackerman Avenue underpass being built.

Fred Arndt captured this summer day at the border of Fair Lawn and Glen Rock, on Maple Avenue, on June 20, 1938 at 1:55 p.m. (Donated by Norma Hibbard, Arndt's sister.)

Baseball was a popular pastime in Glen Rock. Fred Arndt photographed his friends Frank Daly (at bat) and Roger Probert at Tigers Field (located at the corner of Maple and Glen Avenues), on Saturday, April 8, 1938, at 11:15 a.m. (Donated by Norma Hibbard, Arndt's sister.)

The Mugwumps were a local team, and Charles J. Haeberle was one of the team's best players. This photograph was taken on April 23, 1938. Such local teams and competitions were the beginning of the Athletic Club, which is still in existence. (Courtesy of Dorothy Becica, Haeberle's sister.)

Glen Rockers Warren Merboth and Chester Decker were two young men who achieved national recognition as soaring pilots. Both began the hobby at an early age and eventually received the highest ranking. Decker became the National Soaring Champion in 1936 and went on to win additional titles. Merboth placed second in the National Soaring Championship and also went on to win top rankings at other competitions. On October 7, 1939, the men were honored with a tribute in Glen Rock. The day included a parade, band concert, addresses by "America's World War Ace" Eddie Rickenbacker, Governor Moore, and Representative Thomas, and a gliding exhibition by the honorees.

Residents have always taken pride in the appearance of landscaping and gardens. For some, it was a hobby that they enjoyed through the Glen Rock Garden Club. Members offered plants for sale on July 5, 1941.

One winter hobby during the 1920s was cross-country skiing over the Ridgewood Country Club golf course located off Lincoln Avenue in Glen Rock. (Courtesy of Marjorie LaForge.)

American Legion Post 145 produced *Legion Scandals* from 1930 to 1942 and 1946 to 1966. The *Nine O'clock Revue* replaced the productions in 1967. This photograph is of one of the casts of *Legion Scandals* in the early 1930s.

This is the cast of the 1938 *Legion Scandals*, held February 24–26 at Central School.

Many Glen Rock children took part in *Tom Thumb's Wedding*, which was held in the auditorium of the Community Church. Pageants were a common form of entertainment. (Courtesy of Betty Keffer Hall, second row, ninth from the left.)

School pageants were popular events. This costumed cast of a 1939 to 1940 Central School production represented flowers. (Courtesy of Betty Keffer Hall, top row, seventh from the left.)

George Hubschmitt decorated his automobile for the Fourth of July in Ridgewood in 1925. There were a few local festivities over the next 10 years, but many Glen Rockers went to Ridgewood for holiday fun. In 1935, the Glen Rock Parent Teacher Association sponsored a celebration. No organized celebration occurred for the next four years.

George Hubschmitt proudly hitched up his horses and pulled this float in the first Glen Rock Independence Day Association (IDA) Parade in 1939.

The 1939 IDA Parade marched down Rock Road from the Rock to borough hall. Automobiles remained parked, and paradegoers stood in the street to watch the participants go by.

George Hubschmitt's horses pulled his wagon, which was decorated for the 1940 IDA Parade.

The 1942 IDA Parade had numerous bicycles and pedal-powered toys decorated in a patriotic theme.

Rain did not prevent troops housed in nearby barracks from participating in the 1942 IDA Parade.

The women of the Canteen marched in the 1942 IDA Parade and had a booth on the Central School grounds during the day's activities.

This float in the 1942 IDA Parade advertised war bonds and stamps. In addition, mailings were made to Glen Rock residents in an effort to sell the bonds and stamps.

The 1942 IDA Parade ended at borough hall, as had the parades in the past. The crowd listened to dignitaries' speeches, songs, and presentations.

IDA Parade participants of 1942 filled the borough hall grounds and patriotically saluted the flag.

The 1942 Fourth of July celebration on the Central School grounds included this booth sponsored by the parents and teachers of Central School.

Jane Kuna makes her best effort to win the famous handleless rolling-pin throw. The contest was one of the special events during the 1942 Fourth of July fair.

Glen Rock Volunteer Fire Department member Samuel Anthony Nardo is pictured here with his daughter, the Ladies Auxiliary mascot, Harriet Nardo Riley, and David Kuiper posing at the Fourth of July fair.

At the 1942 Fourth of July fair, Borden's Ice Cream, a local business, sponsored a booth that featured its endorsement by the Dionne quintuplets.

Fairgoers cheer on the girls as they compete in a race.

The men's race was made challenging by making the competitors balance a milk bottle on their heads.

Family and friends on the sidelines view the boys' race.

Couples compete in the wheelbarrow race.

World War II made it necessary for the borough to participate in civil defense and disaster control exercises. Civil defense air-raid warden, Robert D. Parker, took this 1943 photograph. It was taken in the Civil Defense Control Center in the municipal building. The members of the Civil Defense Committee seen here are, from left to right, Edward Tilghman, Charles Buhlmann, Sam Parks (police captain), unidentified, and Ted Torrens. (Courtesy of Richard B. Parker, Robert D. Parker's son.)

Over 500 residents attended the July 4, 1943 ceremonies dedicating the Honor Roll of Glen Rock for local men and women serving in World War II. The original monument had 418 names listed and some names were added later. It was wooden and deteriorated over time. The monument was replaced in 1965 by a memorial to those Glen Rock residents who lost their lives serving our country in World War II and the Korean War. Pictured here are, from left to right, Lt. Victor W. Simons (U.S. Navy), John J. Kelly, Mayor W.T. Ludlum, Leo E. Honore, Walter Heebner, Carl Kemm Loven (memorial's designer), Rev. John E. Bailey, Msgr. Edward F. Kirk, Mrs. Arthur Hertter, and Comdr. William A. McHale (U.S. Navy).

Four

YEARS OF GROWTH
1947 THROUGH 1959

The Rock was featured in many floats in the Independence Day Association's 1954 parade, the year the borough celebrated its 60th anniversary. The East Coleman Property Owners Association float is shown at the corner of Andover Terrace and Franklin Place. (Donated by Paul and Diane Herrlett.)

By 1954, the municipal building accommodated borough offices, a police area, and a library wing, which housed a children's library on the lower level and main library on the second level. Organizations used rooms within the building for meetings.

The Glen Rock Volunteer Ambulance Corps was founded in 1951. The groundbreaking for the headquarters took place in 1953.

The Glen Rock Volunteer Ambulance Corps had modern 1951 equipment with which they served the community. The ambulance is parked in front of White's Service Center, a Gulf station on Maple Avenue, now the site of Kilroy's offices.

In the early 1950s, the Glen Rock Volunteer Fire Department received two new fire trucks. ("Glen Rock, A Self Portrait," League of Women Voters of Glen Rock, 1954. Photograph by Morris H. Jaffe.)

On Monday, June 18, 1956, all of the borough's emergency personnel were put to the test when the Leone Lumber and Supply Company burned. By Tuesday morning, all that remained of business were a few cinder-block walls. This view is from the Bergen Line at Rock Road.

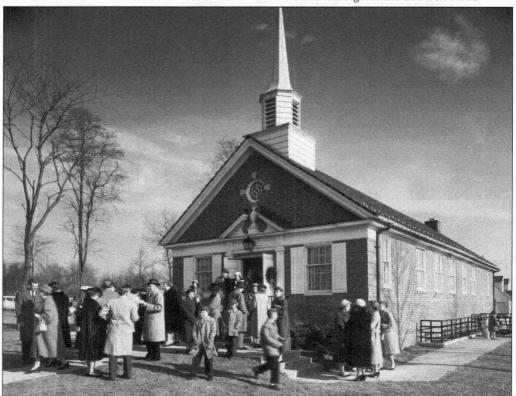

The Good Shepherd Lutheran Church began worship services on January 5, 1947, in the municipal building. In 1953, the church opened its doors at the corner of Rock Road and Ackerman Avenue. As the congregation grew, the original structure was added on to several times over the years. (Courtesy of the Good Shepard Lutheran Church.)

One of the original three hotels in town, the Wagoner became Monarch Motors and Robert Hatchett's Insurance office. This is a 1953 photograph of the site at the northeast corner of Maple Avenue and Harristown Road.

The municipal pool was the dream of a group of Glen Rock youth. They began by talking to local merchant George Betterbed of Excel Cleaners, who suggested a petition. Their campaign gained the support of many civic leaders and opened in 1951. (Courtesy of Lewis W. Dunham.)

Glen Rockers wanted their own post office as early as 1913. Until 1920, residents had to use Ridgewood's post office, as the postmaster in Buffalo, New York, refused to accept mail addressed to Glen Rock. The Smith-Singer Building housed a branch of the Ridgewood Post Office for several years. In 1939, it moved to Thielke's Drug Store on Rock Road. The exact location of the substation during the 20 years prior is not documented. This photograph was taken on June 13, 1959, the day the Glen Rock Post Office was dedicated.

The Rock Road business district grew after World War II. This 1954 photograph shows few empty lots between the two railroad tracks. ("Glen Rock, A Self Portrait," League of Women Voters of Glen Rock, 1954.)

More and more commuters to New York City moved into Glen Rock for an easy commute, good schools, and a beautiful setting. ("Glen Rock, A Self Portrait," League of Women Voters of Glen Rock, 1954. Photograph by Donald A. Sommers.)

More commuting residents meant fewer farms. The DeBoer Farm was the last of Glen Rock's farms. This 1958 photograph was taken at Harristown Road, east of the Main Line Railroad.

Glen Rock Mayor Frederick A. Demarest joined Clarence N. Malone, acting mayor of Ridgewood, to make the first dial service telephone calls in the region. The service started at midnight, January 9, 1954.

Main Street Park's bell states, "This Bell, Symbolic of Freedom is the gift of the Navy Department to the Borough of Glen Rock, December 1954 from the destroyer USS Lang (DD 399) a veteran of ten operations, World War II: Named in Memory of Seaman John Lang, USN, New Brunswick, New Jersey, whose courageous action aboard USS Wasp helped win War 1812, Dedicated May 30th 1955."

Civic-minded residents raised funds for a variety of events. Seen here are, from left to right, Mabel Hubschmitt, Catherine Foley, Marjorie Uhl, Florence Hoogs, and Jane Craig as they work on posters for a 1954 bake sale to benefit the Glen Rock nativity scene.

Summer programs in the borough's parks offered arts and crafts for vacationing students. Marguerite Seybolt, a Glen Rock teacher, assisted students making potholders during August 1954. (Courtesy of Jean Seybolt Rey, Marguerite's daughter.)

Many adults and children were active in scouting. On Memorial Day, 1958, Glen Rock Brownie Troop No. 55 had a "Flying Up" ceremony, where the Brownies were welcomed into the Girl Scouts. (Courtesy of Donna Smith Nihen, center.)

Please return to:

AMERICAN HOUSEWIVES ORGANIZED, INC.
Glen Rock, N. J.

I agree to cooperate wholeheartedly with our national government and refrain from scare buying for the duration of the Korean crisis or other Communistic disorders threatening peace.

I will fight inflation and purchase only my fair share of food and merchandise for current family needs.

Should rationing become necessary, I shall not patronize black markets and will report their existence to proper authorities.

Name

Date   Address

On October 8, 1946, Gloria Bartlett of Glen Rock began American Housewives Organized, Inc. (AHO). The organization's goal was to "promote, by lawful means, any activity having for its object the better of conditions affecting the American home!" Newspapers and radio carried the AHO message. This postcard was issued so that housewives could pledge support. (*Housewives News,* 1948–1949.)

The annual IDA Parade continued to receive support from all facets of the community. The western theme of the 1947 parade was celebrated. This was the first-place winning entry.

Children decorated their bicycles for the annual parade. Some dressed appropriately in western wear.

The Byrd School Brownie Troop marched in the 1947 IDA Parade.

After the parade, Glen Rockers enjoyed the western theme all day at the fair. The Round-Up Milk Bar and Bass Brook Trading Post were just two of the many booths that kept visitors fed and entertained.

Uncle Sam made an appearance in the 1948 IDA Parade.

The blood bank was organized to assist Glen Rock residents but donated to national causes when needed. This 1951 float was created by American Legion Post No. 145.

The Rock supported an Olympic torch runner on this 1952 IDA float.

The 1954 IDA Parade float sponsored by the library featured the well-known Lyla Connell sitting among the children she read to during various programs and story times.

IDA Paradegoers enjoyed the music of the Central School Orchestra in 1954.

Good Shepard Lutheran Church's float in the 1954 IDA Parade proudly displays a picture of the new church.

Grace Mitchel holds high the "Harding Road Gang" sign that introduced the first entry the neighborhood had in an IDA Parade. The 1954 entry was a larger-than-life firecracker followed by Harding Road residents of all ages.

Glen Rock teachers entered this float for a mid-1950s IDA Parade.

The blood bank had a presence in many IDA Parades. Two unidentified women accompany driver Dorothy Demarest.

Flag waving was always a part of a parade. Waiting for the 1957 Memorial Day Parade, Donna Smith stands on Rock Road near the intersection with Glen Avenue. (Courtesy of Donna Smith Nihen.)

A marching band goes past Glen Rock stores during the 1957 Memorial Day Parade down Rock Road. (Courtesy of Donna Smith Nihen.)

The League of Women Voters of Glen Rock sponsored this float in the 1957 IDA Parade.

Celebrating the anniversary of the New Jersey Constitution, this float was in the 1957 IDA Parade. (Courtesy of Donna Smith Nihen.)

Conservation was the theme of this 1958 float that listed "Smokey the Bear's Commandments." Smokey and the cubs are unidentified.

Clara Coleman taught first and second grades in Glen Rock for 36 years, from September 1911 to June 1947. In 1950, a wing of the junior high school, which was being used for kindergarten through sixth grades, was named in her honor. In 1954, the new elementary school was named for her. This photograph, given to the school by Robert Buckalew, shows Coleman's last class, the class of 1947. (Courtesy of Dr. Connolly, principal of Clara E. Coleman School.)

The Clara E. Coleman School was constructed on the site of Hopper farms of the past. Years ago, Scotch Runner strawberries were grown and harvested in small baskets made by the farm families by the fireside during the winter. Just outside the school grounds is the Hopper Family Burying Ground. The tombstones and farmland can be seen in this 1952 photograph of the site. The two children playing in the background are unidentified; Karen Peterson Ferranti is in the foreground.

Each new school experienced firsts. Principal Robert H. Seitzer took this photograph of Charles L. Dages II on September 20, 1954. Charles was the first student with a birthday in the new school. (Courtesy of Helen M. Dages, Charles's mother.)

Saint Catharine Interparochial School was planned and built in 1952 and 1953. It opened its door to approximately 500 kindergarten through eighth grade students on October 13, 1953. This photograph was taken on September 7, 1953.

Overcrowding in Central School and the Clara E. Coleman School created the need for the Alexander Hamilton School. The elementary school wing of the junior high school, once known as the Clara E. Coleman wing, was referred to as the Alexander Hamilton Elementary School during the year prior to the opening of the new school. This photograph was taken on March 9, 1958.

Alexander Hamilton Elementary School's first kindergarten class poses with books open on April 21, 1959. Mrs. Snyder's students are, from left to right, as follows: (front row) unidentified, Steven "Barry" Speck, Suzie Hoagland, unidentified, Debbie Rinbrand, Melinda Cake, and Ken Gordon; (back row) Douglas Cadell, Jon Mersereau, Kathy Kort, Alice Sue Adams, Pamela Smith, Joanne Leggett, Phillip Ferraro, Alan Jurewicz, and Frederick Doot. (Courtesy of Pamela Smith Speck.)

The dedication of the Glen Rock High School took place on Wednesday, November 14, 1956. Following speeches by local dignitaries and an address by the provost of Rutgers University, the new facility was opened to the public. The original high school had two wings, which were one story in height, plus a two-story classroom wing. Both the junior and senior high schools used the auditorium, gymnasium, and special purpose rooms. Outdoors, the junior and senior high schools shared a football field surrounded by a quarter-mile track, soccer fields, softball and hardball diamonds, and hard-surface play areas.

. Dedication Program .

Glen Rock High School

Hamilton Avenue

Glen Rock, New Jersey

WEDNESDAY, NOVEMBER 14, 1956

8:00 P. M.

Open House — following program

The Green Thumb Club is just one example of the pride students took in their new high school. Members were responsible for the plants inside the school. They held clean-up days and assisted with landscaping the school. Participants seen here are, from left to right, the following: (first row) C. Stucky, L. Connolly, E. Kirchof, and advisor Charles Winter; (second row) R. Russack, L. Paterson, M. Hawes, M. Ball, K. Moran, P. Steele, and U. Obeda; (third row) J. Caron, D. Lambert, S. Anderson, and G. Stiles.

The 1958–1959 Math Team competed with students from 19 other high schools. They are pictured with a giant slide rule in the 1959 Glenconian. Pictured are, from left to right, B.J. Fleming, G. Krech, B. Dovey, D. Doviak, N. Wade, advisor Jack Leonard, B.Behn, G. Berzak, A. Allen, S. Knecht, J. Sundberg, and G. Bovenizer.

The 1959 Glenconian lists the Boys' Tumbling Club as under the direction of Carl Swanson. In addition to performing basic stunts, they were known for creating their own exercises and stunts. The members are, from left to right, as follows: (first row) J. Rector, S. Murphy, R. Meyer, D. Brevet, D. Lichtenheim, J. Sinkway, and B. Lee; (second row) C. Swanson, B Prichard, J. Wilcox, and D. Yates; (third row) R. Ray.

A moonlight sleigh ride was the theme of the holiday ball held at the high school in December 1958. These unidentified couples were dressed for the formal occasion.

The Glen Rock High School had its first graduating class 65 years after the borough's founding families decided that incorporating was the only way to provide quality education for their children and keep them close to home. The Class of 1959 contained 136 students. This program included the Alma Mater:

Praise to thee, O Alma Mater
Praise to thee, O Glen Rock High
We salute thee, Alma Mater
With our banners raised on high
As champion of Justice, Honor, and Right
Leading us onward to glory and might;
These our years 'neath thy guidance and care
Have given us this unity we always will share.
Your truth and honor, we'll always defend
Keeping our school firm as the Rock in the Glen.

FIRST ANNUAL

COMMENCEMENT

GLEN ROCK HIGH SCHOOL

Glen Rock, New Jersey

June 15, 1959

Officer William Doot stops traffic for schoolchildren returning home from Byrd School in 1954. ("Glen Rock, A Self Portrait," League of Women Voters of Glen Rock, 1954. Photograph by Morris H. Jaffe.)

Printed in the USA
CPSIA information can be obtained
at www.ICGtesting.com
LVHW081745200923
758542LV00024B/51